SUPER BOWL CHAMPIONS
WASHINGTON REDSKINS

RUNNING BACK
ALFRED MORRIS

SUPER BOWL CHAMPIONS

WASHINGTON REDSKINS

AARON FRISCH

CREATIVE EDUCATION

Published by Creative Education
P.O. Box 227, Mankato, Minnesota 56002
Creative Education is an imprint of The Creative Company
www.thecreativecompany.us

Design and production by Blue Design
Art direction by Rita Marshall
Printed in the United States of America

Photographs by Corbis (Bettmann, Wally McNamee),
Getty Images (Bernstein Associates, Rob Carr, Mark
Cunningham, Nate Fine/NFL, Focus on Sport, Mark Gail/
MCT, Jed Jacobsohn, John McDonnell/The Washington
Post, Al Messerschmidt, Jonathan Newton/The
Washington Post, Vito Palmisano, Pro Football Hall of
Fame/NFL, Robert Riger, Allen Dean Steele/NFL, Rob
Tringali/SportsChrome)

Library of Congress Cataloging-in-Publication Data
Frisch, Aaron.
Washington Redskins / Aaron Frisch.
p. cm. — (Super bowl champions)
Includes index.
Summary: An elementary look at the Washington
Redskins professional football team, including its
formation in Boston in 1932, most memorable players,
Super Bowl championships, and stars of today.
ISBN 978-1-60818-389-0
1. Washington Redskins (Football team)—History—
Juvenile literature. I. Title.

GV956.W3F753 2014
796.332'6409753—dc23   2013014826

First Edition
9 8 7 6 5 4 3 2 1

DEFENSIVE TACKLE
ALBERT HAYNESWORTH

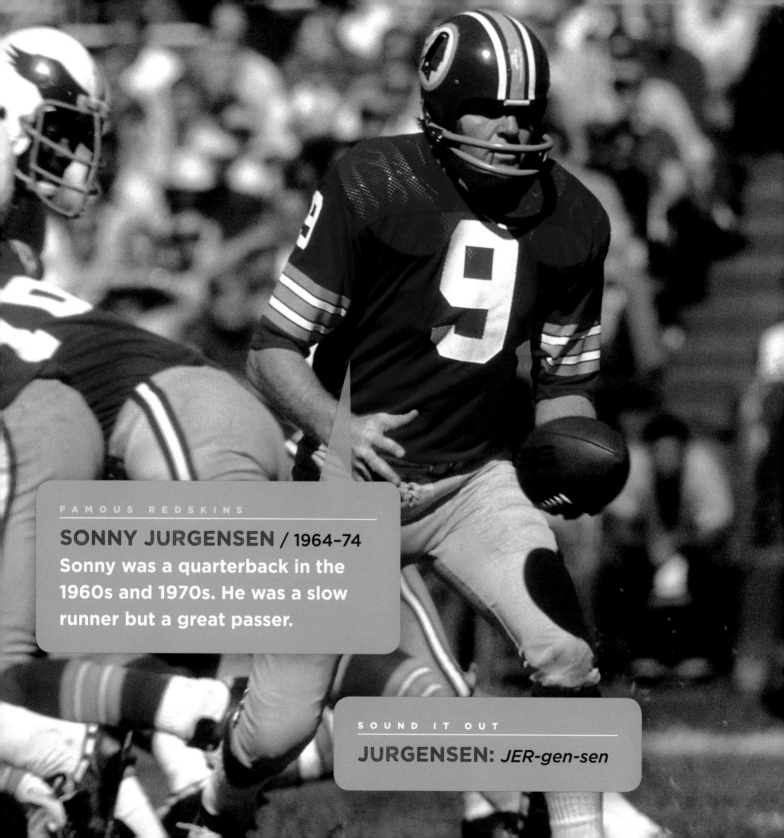

SONNY JURGENSEN / 1964–74

Sonny was a quarterback in the 1960s and 1970s. He was a slow runner but a great passer.

SOUND IT OUT

JURGENSEN: *JER-gen-sen*

TABLE OF CONTENTS

BOBBY MITCHELL / 1962-68
Bobby was a speedy running back. He helped his team by returning kicks and punts, too.

BRAVES AND REDSKINS

In 1937, a football team called the Boston Braves moved to Washington, D.C. The team got new uniforms and a new name. The Washington Redskins have been playing ever since!

1942 CHAMPION REDSKINS

REDSKINS 14
WIN - 6

9

WELCOME TO WASHINGTON

Washington, D.C., is a small area of land that is the **capital** of the United States. Washington has a lot of famous buildings. Many people like to visit Washington.

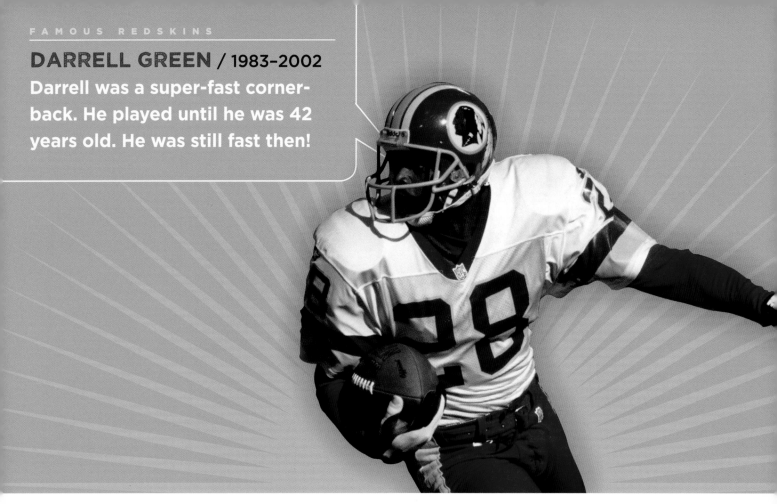

DARRELL GREEN / 1983–2002
Darrell was a super-fast corner-back. He played until he was 42 years old. He was still fast then!

TOUGH RIVALS

The Washington Redskins play in a **division** that has some of the National Football League's (NFL) oldest teams. The Redskins' biggest **rivals** are the Dallas Cowboys.

CLINTON PORTIS / 2004-10

Clinton was a small but tough running back. He ran for almost 10,000 yards in his NFL **career**.

SAM HUFF

THE REDSKINS' STORY

The Redskins played their first five seasons as the Braves. After they moved to Washington, quarterback Sammy Baugh helped them win NFL championships in 1937 and 1942.

The Redskins added new stars like strong linebacker Sam Huff. But they lost many games in the 1950s and 1960s.

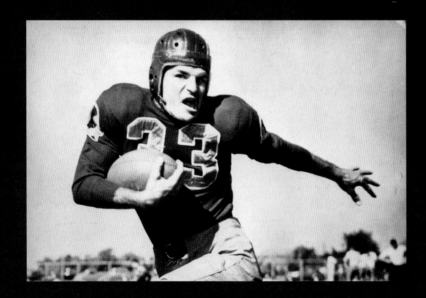

SAMMY BAUGH

15

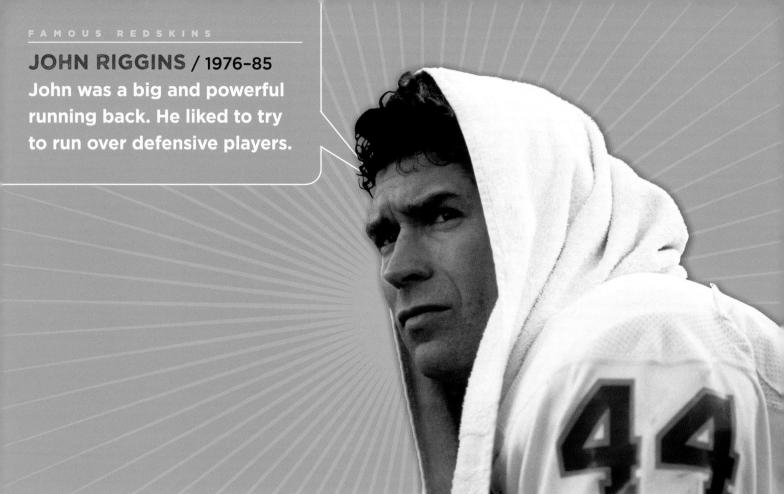

JOHN RIGGINS / 1976–85

John was a big and powerful running back. He liked to try to run over defensive players.

The Redskins got to their first Super Bowl after the 1972 season. They lost that game, but soon new coach Joe Gibbs made them a better team.

JOE GIBBS

"I just loved the game, loved to play, loved being out there."
—ART MONK

The Redskins had a lot of big, strong offensive linemen in the 1980s. Fans called them "The Hogs." Washington won the Super Bowl after the 1982 and 1987 seasons!

Wide receiver Art Monk helped Washington win another championship four seasons later. Stars like fast cornerback Champ Bailey made football fun in Washington after that.

BRIAN ORAKPO / 2009–present

Brian was a strong linebacker. He played in the **Pro Bowl** after his first two NFL seasons.

ORAKPO: *oh-RAK-poh*

By 2013, Washington had many new players like Robert Griffin III. Robert was a fast quarterback nicknamed "RG3." Redskins fans couldn't wait for another Super Bowl!

ROBERT GRIFFIN III

FACTS FILE

CONFERENCE/DIVISION:
National Football
Conference, East Division

TEAM COLORS:
Burgundy and gold

HOME STADIUM:
FedExField

SUPER BOWL VICTORIES:
XVII, January 30, 1983
    27–17 over Miami
    Dolphins
XXII, January 31, 1988
    42–10 over Denver
    Broncos
XXVI, January 26, 1992
    37–24 over Buffalo Bills

NFL WEBSITE FOR KIDS:
http://nflrush.com

DEFENSIVE END
STEPHEN BOWEN

GLOSSARY

capital — a city where the laws for a state or country are made

career — all the years that an athlete plays

division — a group of teams within a league that play many games against each other

Pro Bowl — a special game after the season that only the best NFL players get to play

rivals — teams that play extra hard against each other

INDEX